Gran Canaria

D1635181

Editorial Everest would like to thank you for purchasing this book. It has been created by an extensive and complete publishing team made up of photographers, illustrators and authors specialised in the field of tourism, together with our modern cartography department. Everest guarantees that the contents of this work were completely up to date at the time of going to press, and we would like to invite you to send us any information that helps us to improve our publications, so that we may always offer QUALITY TOURISM.

QUALITY
TOURISM
WITH
EVEREST

Please send your comments to:
Editorial Everest. Dpto. de Turismo
Apartado 339 – 24080 León (Spain)
Or e-mail them to us at turismo@everest.es

Editorial Management: Raquel López Varela

Editorial coordination: Eva María Fernández

Text: Vicente Sánchez Araña

Photographs: Oliviero Daidola, Paolo Tiengo and Orietta Ghersi, Justino Díez

Diagrams: Gerardo Rodera

Diseño de cubierta: Alfredo Anievas

Cartography: © Everest
     Street plan of Las Palmas by Montse Gual

Translated by EURO:TEXT

© EDITORIAL EVEREST, S. A.
Carretera León-La Coruña, km 5 - LEÓN
ISBN: 84-241-0237-1
Legal deposit: LE. 464-2001
Printed in Spain

EDITORIAL EVERGRÁFICAS, S. L.
Carretera León-La Coruña, km 5
LEÓN (Spain)

Gran Canaria

◆ ## LAS PALMAS DE GRAN CANARIA

The Very Noble and Loyal City of Real de Las Palmas de Gran Canaria, as its title has read since 1515, came into being in Spanish and world history on 24 June 1478, the day that Castilian troops, under the sign of the cross, landed on the beaches of the islands and established their Royal Camp near a palm forest (from which the name derived) and a small stream called Guiniguada.

The first Castilian city in the Canary Archipelago which, due to the sense of duty of all the inhabitants of Gran Canaria throughout its history, has become the largest and most populated city in the Canary Autonomous Community. According to the 1992 municipal statistics, Las Palmas has nine districts registered with a population of 355.000 inhabitants on a constructed surface area of 35% of the nearly one hundred square kilometres that lie within the municipal boundaries.

Santa Catalina.

It is a beautiful city open to visitors from all over the world, cosmopolitan and cheerful, which offers the thousands of tourists who visit daily a pleasant, mild climate dominated by delicious breezes from the blue Atlantic which bathes its extraordinary ten kilometres of beaches running from North to South. It is possible for them to walk through the lively avenues or have refreshments at the seaside on winter nights while enjoying a temperature that does not drop below 15 degrees Centigrade.

In the innumerable shops found in the **Calle de Triana**, a street closed to vehicles in the second district of Las Palmas de Gran Canaria, one can acquire costly or simple souvenirs. **Doramas Park** accommodates different specimens of indigenous floral. Hotel Santa Catalina, a building designed in Canarian Style by Miguel Martín Fernández de la Torre is also on the grounds. The Las Palmas Casino is located in this hotel.

The **Plaza de Santa Ana** was the third of the first plazas constructed in the City of Las Palmas de Gran Canaria. It was preceded by the Plazas de San Antón and Los Alamos. Its construction in the dawn of the XVI Century was due to the demands for expansion in the Vegueta neighbourhood, the first urban nucleus in **Las Palmas de Gran Canaria**. This plaza continues to be an obligatory site for the capital's events and celebrations of high social standing. This historic, rectangular plaza is dominated by the City Hall, a neoclassical building, which was inaugurated on 29 April 1856, replacing an earlier structure which was destroyed by fire in 1842. The Episcopal Palace, the Provincial Historical Archives and the Cathedral of Las Palmas are located along the sides of the plaza.

Santa Ana Cathedral though its façade is neoclassical, has a strong Gothic style interior. It was the first Hispanic church built in the Canary Islands.

Columbus' house.

Plaza de Santa Ana.

♦ Plaza de Cairasco with the Literary Section in the background.

Next, two-page view of Las Palmas de Gran Canaria.

The **vicinity of the Port**. The port district is an important urban nucleus full or mercantile vitality. Featuring the outstanding Santa Catalina Park, its streets are lined by banks, warehouses, shops and businesses, hotels, restaurants and all sorts of attractions to delight the passers-by.

The **Castillo de la Luz**, an old fort dating from the end of the XV Century, will soon house a museum, thus realising one of the city's long standing aspirations.

Puerto de la Luz

The *Bahía de la Luz*, the bay with its well distributed and vast docks offers all types of port operations to ships from all over the world. Endowed with all the facilities and services necessary for the thousands of passengers who arrive at our island.

Due to its privileged situation, the Puerto de la Luz y de Las Palmas, the city's harbour, has witnessed many great oceanic enterprises, including Columbus' departure as he set off to discover of the New World.

Playa de las Canteras

This beach is considered one of the best in the world due to its natural features and exceptional location. Its name comes from the nearby sandstone quarries which provided the material for the construction of the first buildings in our city.

Las Palmas de Gran Canaria. Mardi Gras.

"Pueblo Canario" (Canary Island village).

The three kilometre long beach, a crescent of fine, golden sand, is provided by nature with a sand bar two hundred metres long which protects the shore from high waves.

One can enjoy swimming and many other sports in its warm waters by day or night since it is equipped with magnificent illumination.

Playa de Las Canteras. ▶

ARUCAS, FIRGAS Y MOYA

Arucas, Firgas and Moya are three geographic enclaves of great natural beauty in the north of Gran Canaria, each one offering the visitor its particular features. In all three districts one detects a verdant agriculture since the three share a common treasure: the water that is so necessary for our Island.

Arucas, formerly called Arehucas, is known as the Town of Flowers and the Banana Capital.

There is easy access to its mountain and from the summit, on which there is a belvedere restaurant, one can admire a bird's-eye view of the banana plantations which cover the entire region. A visit to the historic centre of the town which includes Gourié Park, the Casa del Marquesado, the Sureda Art Gallery, the Cultural Centre, the Municipal Market, the quarries of blue rock, the Canary rum distilleries and the Cathedral is a must in this old port town on the Gran Canaria Northern Route.

Thirty kilometres from the capital one finds **Moya**, also known as Villa Verde (Green Town). The parish church is surprising due to its collection of architectural styles though the Colonial is dominant.

The Neo-Gothic **Basilica of Arucas** was built between 1909 and 1977 with stone from its own quarries following the plans of Manuel Vega Mar, a Catalonian architect and disciple of Gaudí.

The legendary **Villa de Moya**, cradle of warriors and poets, famous for its laurel forest and exuberant fronds is also renowned for its delicious cakes.

Twenty-five kilometres from Las Palmas de Gran Canaria we come upon **Firgas** situated on the peak of a mountain whose inhabitants' houses are harmoniously scattered over its slopes.

The different vantage points for contemplating picturesque landscape afford interesting views of white haciendas and typical Canary Island houses. The most famous mineral water in our autonomous Community is found here under the denomination of *Agua de Firgas*.

View of Firgas.

GUÍA, GÁLDAR Y AGAETE

Guía, Gáldar and Agaete: two towns and a village that comprise the northwest of Gran Canaria. **Santa María de Guía**, a cultured and hard-working town which converted its old hermitage into a large church in the neoclassical and baroque styles, was founded at the end of the XV Century by the conqueror of Gran Canaria from Madrid, Sancho de Vargas Machuca. The sculptor Luján Pérez (1756-1815) and Don Pedro Gordillo y Ramos, Representative and President of the Cortes Españolas (the Spanish Parliament) from 1810 to 1813 are among its most outstanding "Illustrious Sons." The handcrafted products of this town are quite famous. Among them is the delicious cheese, *queso de flor*.

Gáldar. The progressive and dynamic town of **Santiago de los Caballeros de Gáldar** has the honour of having been the old capital of Gran Canaria and the Courst of the Guanarteme Dynasty kings. Among its many attractions are extraordinary archaeological sites such as the original *Cueva Pintada* (Painted Cave).

Agaete. The village of Agaete is the holder of one of the most picturesque and valuable jewels of Gran Canaria: the triptych of the Virgen de las Nieves (Our Lady of the Snows), a work of the Flemish painter Joos Van Clever (1518-1520).

The Pines of Gáldar. Exuberant vegetation appears on the volcanic ash of the young crater of recent eruption, about three thousand years old, which rises to a height of 1,700

metres above sea level. On its slopes the temperature ranges from 10º C. in winter and 40º C. in summer. Mount Teide emerges from the Atlantic like a great grounded fortress.

The white fishing village of **Agaete** offers strongly rooted popular traditions such as the Fiesta de la Rama. The

Upper left, parish church of Santa María de Guía.

Above, View of Gáldar.

Huerto de las Flores (The Flower Garden) stands out from the natural beauty of great ecological value which one encounters here. And down below on the beach are the typical restaurants which invite the traveller to try the traditional *caldo de pescado con mojo verde* (Fish stews with green sauce), *queso tierno* (soft cheese), and *gofio* (a corn meal porridge).

Caressed by the resonant Atlantic's white-capped turquoise waves, the impressive geological formation called the **Finger of God** (*El Dedo de Dios*) in stands in the shade of the buttresses of Tirma.

◀ Dedo de Dios (Finger of God).   ◀ Ermita de las Nieves (Shrine of the Snows).   ◀ View of Agaete.

TEROR, VALLESECO AND ARTENARA

The district of **Teror** is found 21 kilometres from the capital, **Las Palmas de Gran Canaria**, on the route through the centre of the island. The town itself, dedicated to St. Mary, features a basilica which houses the statue of *Nuestra Señora del Pino* (Our Lady of the Pine), patroness of the Dioceses of the Canary Islands. Its Feast Day is the 8th of September. This historic town is located amidst ample valleys and gently rolling hills at an altitude of 543 metres. On the route climbing towards the heights of Gran Canaria on country-road number C-812 is **Valleseco**, made up of three luxuriant valleys with native plants only to be found in these latitudes which cover the reddish earth with gold nearly all year. The yellow *giralda* (C.myconis) contrasts with the blue *jopo* (O.crenata) while, mid-mountain, the gigantic walnuts vie with the black poplar that masters the blue skies of Gran Canaria. The best illustration of the peaceful atmosphere pervading

the heights of the island is found at **Artenara**, a village boasting magnificent landscape and truly ancestral architecture, some of its inhabitants still living in caves, the dwelling-places of their forefathers, the ancient Canary Islanders. From here we are afforded an extraordinary view of Mount Teide, clearly visible in the distance over the sea. The different renovations to which the **Basilica of Nuestra Señora del Pino** (Our Lady of the Pine) has been subjected throughout four centuries has left it with such different architectural styles as Gothic, baroque, neoclassical and Mudéjar. The 24 metre high tower is clearly influenced by the Portuguese Manualino style. The epitome of handcrafted woodwork is found in the typical balconies of the buildings in **Teror.** The Canarian cabinetmakers and woodturners have left a wide sample of their noble art. The principal street is full of examples of the woodturners trade done in material extracted from the heart of Canarian pines called tea. The Cistercian Monastery and the

View of Teror.

Evening falls with Roque Nublo and the Teide in the background.

residence of the Dominican Nuns with its Neo-Romanesque arcade constructed with the blue Gran Canarian rock and other noble native materials endow this town with prestige and distinction. It is not for nothing that this is the town of the Patron Saint of Gran Canaria.

Evidence of the prosperous agricultural past is still found in the old farmhouses where a profusion of no longer used utensils and farm equipment rest.

Nearby lie spots such as **Barranco de la Virgen**, formerly property of the Patroness, *Cortijo de Osorio*, San Matías and *Balcón de Zamora* which offer a splendid panorama of native flora amidst which the typical white houses are seen to rise up. Teror's famous table water, recipient of an award at the Brussels Exposition of 1910 for recognized medicinal qualities, is bottled at the *Fuente Agria*.

Forests of Canary pine (pinus canariensis) lord over the summits of the Gran Canaria Mountains. Thousands of them owe their existence to the great reforestation done during the last thirty years.

Comparative studies of fossils from the Himalayas allow botanists to affirm that our pines' nearest relative was found in that far off land during the Tertiary Age.

The exuberant verdure which proliferates in the countryside belie the name of the town known as **Valleseco** (Dry Valley). Its green orchards, punctuated with the varied colours of the delicious fruit to be harvested, give it a singular beauty.

Artenara is Gran Canaria's highest town and can be called the Island's balcony. From these heights, the visitor not only contemplates the beautiful nearby views, but beyond the blue horizon that surrounds him, the silhouette of colossal Mount Teide can be seen dominating the seas that form its natural boundary.

From the heights of **Artenara** the play of light on the sea and rocks causes one to pause and meditate on the prodigality of nature on Gran Canaria. From here dreamlike landscapes are offered to the visitor while, way down in the bowels of the Earth, the Virgin in her grotto awaits the daily arrival of innumerable visitors.

The pilgrimage in honour of Our Lady of the Pine at Teror.

Casa de los Patronos, atrium.

◀ Valleseco   ▶ Arts and crafts from Teror.

Artenara.

Two-page spread
overleaf, Tejeda and
Roque Bentayga.

Country house
in Ayacata. ➤

Cruz de Tejeda.   Roque Nublo.

TEJEDA

Words nearly profane the ancient silence of these mountain peaks which rose from the depths of the sea approximately 14 million years ago. The first cataclysms, which occurred in the Miocene Age, created the oldest geological formation on the island of Gran Canaria. The monumental Tejeda crater, whose rocks and volcanic ash occupy the space of a thousand cubic kilometres, is attributed to this period. And so other cycles of eruption were initiated until the roundness of our island and its appendage, La Isleta (The Islet), only 3,000 years old, were formed. From these heights we are afforded a grandiose view of deep ravines and arrogant, perfectly delineated mountains like those of the *Pechos de la Cumbre* (Breasts of the Summit), 1,950 metres in altitude and the maximum height above sea level on Gran Canaria. Glorious and historic landmarks in the history of the Island bear witness to the life and customs of the prehistoric Canarian population.

Amongst others, there are the *Cuevas del Rey* (King's Caves), *Almorgarén del Bentayga* and Mount Umiaga where aborigines, in union with the *Harimaguadas* (ancient Canarian priestesses), the *Guanartemes* (Kings) and *Faycanes* (sourcerers), made offerings of milk and honey in honour of the god Alcorac.

Our fauna includes some endangered species. This is the case of the Falco tinnunculus canariensis of the falcon family, known as the common kestrel, a beneficial bird in agriculture due to the large quantities of rodents it consumes.

The **Parador de Tejeda**, an hotel in a beautiful building constructed in native wood and local stone, is located among the island's sunny peaks. It was designed by the Canarian architect Miguel Martín Fernández de la Torre. The surprising view seen from its ample terraces leaves one with an unforgettable memory. Outstanding among the immense mountain ranges is the glorious Roque Bentayga, witness through the centuries to the epic deeds performed by Canarians and Castilians in times past. It was here that the Faycán de Teide, on addressing the invading troops, uttered the immortal words, "Gran Canaria has not died! Look at her up there in the peaks that soar so high!"

Native sports at the foot of los Roques.

SANTA BRÍGIDA, SAN MATEO AND VALSEQUILLO

La Vega de Santa Brígida, today a small town, is found on the central route at only 14 kms from Las Palmas de Gran Canaria. It was the residential area of an English community that settled on our island. To them we owe the blend of rural architecture and exotic Neo-Gothic style buildings. Their well cared for gardens form an aristocratic setting rich with decorative plants.

Near the Villa de Santa Brígida is **San Mateo**, a cattle ranching locality where the Canarian, in constant battle with adversity, wisely substituted traditional agriculture with modern arboriculture and vegetable crops which earn considerable profits.

The livestock is distinguished by the exemplary beauty of the local animals. The popular flea market, open every Saturday and Sunday of the year, is quite famous.

Valsequillo, located in the southwest of Gran Canaria only a few kilometres from the town of Telde, is a beautiful, picturesque town composed of exuberant valleys covered with verdure. It is here that the "Almond Blossom Route" to Tejeda begins.

The inland towns on the island provide farmers and craftsmen with fertile land for the successful practice of their professional activities. Both groups have managed to maintain the heritage handed down to them by their forefathers despite the constant battle against a lack of means and a depressed economy.

La Vega de Santa Brígida, formerly Satautejo, was the first urban nucleus in the central zone of Gran Canaria. The first hermitage in this spacious territory bordered by Tejeda, a town prolific with Canarian flora and fauna, was built on its soil.

Valsequillo, a beautiful valley in the west-central mountain ranges only a few kilometres from Telde, offers an enviable panorama due to the diversity and exuberance of the valleys, especially Tenteniguada, a floral symphony of almond trees along the route to Tejeda.

Santa Brígida.

Golf course.

Melenara beach.

View of Telde.

TELDE, INGENIO AND AGÜIMES

Telde, also known as the *City of the Faycanes*, has the honour of having been the first episcopal seat in the Canary Archipelago. Demographically it is the second largest city on the island. It shares the location of the Gran Canaria Airport with **Villa de Ingenio**. Today it is an industrial city of the first order, but even so, its varied agriculture with banana plantations, vegetable crops and profuse variety of fruits, has not lost its fame.

Ingenio owes its name to the rudimentary sugar industry and the cultivation of sugar-cane which were commenced in 1527 by Juan de Matos in the Valle Real de Aguatona, which, at that time, belonged to **Villa de Agüimes**, today an independent district.

Agüimes, which extends from Gando to Temisas, was granted to the Bishop of the Canary Islands by Ferdinand and Isabella, the Catholic Monarchs, as an honorarium for his participation in the conquest of Gran Canaria. Its hegemony was lost in 1819 when it was separated from the township of Ingenio.

Both towns have their own life and a promising future - Agüimes with its industrial zone and Ingenio with its agriculture and handcrafts.

The beautiful **Church of San Juan Bautista in Telde** (1483 - 1539) was constructed in a Neogothic-Mudéjar style. Singularly typical neighbourhoods such as *San Antonio* and *San Francisco* are found in the **outskirts of Telde**, and on its coastline are residential areas as well as peaceful Gando Beach and bustling **Melenara Beach**.

Within the Villa de Ingenio area are localities like **Carrizal,** cradle of poets, historians and important soldiers one of whom was General Morales who, through his own merits, went from apprentice salt merchant to Field

Open-work embroidery at "El Molino".

Marshal of the Spanish Army in Venezuela and ended his career as Captain General and Regent of the Court of Canaria.

The purest example of Canarian *calado* (embroidery openwork) is found in this district in the Gil Espino family, famed specialists in this handicraft which they have inherited from their ancestors.

Without losing its traditions sources, the economy of **Agüimes** has opened its doors to the exterior by constructing the island's largest and most important industrial zone on its coast.

A first-class commercial dock will soon be available for use and will channel the exports of the nearby industries. **Arinaga Beach** is well prepared for all types of water sports.

View of Agüimes.

Church of Ingenio.

«La Fortaleza» museum.

SANTA LUCÍA, SAN BARTOLOMÉ DE TIRAJANA AND MOGÁN

The coastal zone of **Santa Lucía de Tirajana** is outstanding for its production of tomatoes, 10 million crates a year, as well as for its famous *Pozo Izquierdo* Beach. The peaks offer impressive views of great beauty, framed by the buttresses of the Tirajana crater. To its unequalled agriculture and copious variety of fruit trees is added the loveliness of blue skies studded with palm and olive trees. Capital of the island's history, Santa Lucía de Tirajana guards on its summit the legendary Ansite Rock where Gran Canaria was incorporated into Castile on 29 April, 1483.

In the distribution of natural gifts to our island, **San Bartolomé de Tirajana** was blessed with the formation of spacious beaches of golden sand which are caressed by the warm, soft waves that bathe an arc 35 kms long. Complementing this natural gift are the sand dunes, the Oasis and the *Charca de Maspalomas*. The hotel complexes offer a warm welcome and efficient service to the thousands of travellers who daily arrive for a visit.

There in the distant blue of the coastline, one can see **Mogán,** an exceptional tourist resort with more than eight sand beaches, three ports and ten tourist areas.

San Rafael de Vecindario, set in the coastal zone of the district of Santa Lucía de Tirajana.

Views of de Fataga and San Bartolomé de Tirajana.

Rambling up and down the Fataga ravine.

Surfing at Pozo Izquierdo.

Playa del Inglés: night time view.

Playa del Inglés. Ecumenical Church (above) and wide view (below).

La **Fortaleza** (The Fortress) of Santa Lucía de Tirajana with its original façade is now the Museum of Archaeology, Anthropology and Ethnography, where valuable pieces from the Canarian aborigine and posterior cultures are on display.

Santa Lucía de Tirajana, capital of the district, offers the visitor a view of its beautiful church with eclectic, neoclassical lines and the stunning panoramas of its colossal crater.

San Bartolomé de Tirajana, capital of the largest district of Gran Canaria, is situated in the island heights where, together with Santa Lucía de Tirajana, it is encircled by a volcanic crater. A few kilometres along the route to the coast is the Hacienda of **Fataga** and, below, in **Maspalomas**, the beaches of golden sand invite us to swim in their warm waters while the radiant sun caresses our skin.

Religious activities of different denominations are celebrated at the **the Playa del Inglés** (The Englishman's Beach) Ecumenical Church.

At **Palmitos Park in Maspalomas**, the visitor is offered the opportunity to contemplate specimens of the most varied flora and fauna brought from the most distant points of the planet and adapted to our privileged climate.

The **Barranco de Arguineguín** is a ravine that forms the boundary between the districts of San Bartolomé de Tirajana and Mogán. In only a short time Arguineguín has become a very important tourist enclave, and, as if doing honour to its name, an allusion to the tranquility of the sea and its ideal location, has completed the construction of a **fishing harbour in Arguineguín** which has a breakwater 360 metres long and a surface of 200 metres of berths equipped for all classes of light and medium-tonnage ships, including ferries.

To the important tourist attractions which are offered in the Mogán locality of **Arguineguín** must be added the comfortable and well fitted out hotel complexes. The guest not only enjoys a deserved rest, but may also take advantage of the ample beaches of fine sand, spacious avenues and a natural setting which offers an immense variety of exotic plants whose flowers

Maspalomas.
The lighthouse (above, right) and the Mardi Gras (above, left).

Two-page spread overleaf, Playa Amadores.

Maspalomas: a bird's eye view with the dunes in the foreground. ▶

From top to bottom: Canary Island-style wrestling in Veneguera, Palmitos Park and Mundo Aborigen (Native World)

embellish the area with their colours of varied shades.

The town of **Mogán** comprises two very important economic zones. Firstly, the agricultural zone, located in the valley, produces vegetable and

Puerto Rico.

Playa del Cura.

Maritime procession in Mogán.

Taurito.

Anfi de Mar.

Trip through the Soria Ravine.

Mogán.

tropical fruits whose harvest surpasses four thousand metric tonnes per season. And secondly, the coast, with its beaches, tourist complexes and a port capable of mooring 226 pleasure craft and having a line of berths 147 metres long specifically for the use of the vessels of the Fishermen's Guild of Mogán.

SAN NICOLÁS DE TOLENTINO

In the most abrupt region of the Island of Gran Canaria lies the beautiful Valley of San Nicolás de Tolentino whose advantageous situation makes it possible for us to travel right round the island.

The farmers of this beautiful corner of Gran Canaria have converted these lands that were torn from the grasp of feudalism by peasants armed only with the right of having cultivated them during centuries into an emporium of wealth. At least that is how the Government of the Nation understood the situation when in 1927, after several years of litigation, it handed them over to those who had been legally cultivating them. Today that latifundium, in the hands of intelligent cooperative farmers, has managed to produce enormous quantities of vegetables and tomatoes

San Nicolás de Tolentino: different
views of the valley.

for export and dairy products from its
livestock for local consumption.
The mighty nature of the mountains,
the smooth aspect of the plains and
the green of the fields offer the visitor
the opportunity to contemplate an
extraordinary, truly unforgettable
landscape.
Beneath **Tasarte** and **Tasartico,** two
impressive rocky outcrops, nestle
small, cosy typical houses with red tile
roofs and whitewashed façades
surrounded by myriads of native
plants and other species which give a
happy note to such an abrupt, solitary
landscape whose indescribable peace
is conducive to meditation. Under the
exuberant grove of the **Parador
Rubén Díaz,** named after its founder,
right on the beach one can
contemplate gorgeous sunsets with
Mount Teide in the background - a
view that is unique in all Gran Canaria.